AF616670

One Child Sold

Human Trafficking & Rights

Poems by

LARRY JAFFE

salmonpoetry

Published in 2010 by
Salmon Poetry
Cliffs of Moher, County Clare, Ireland
Website: www.salmonpoetry.com
Email: info@salmonpoetry.com

ISBN 978-1-907056-45-1

Cover design: *Gracia Bennish – www.graciacreative.com*
Cover design & typesetting: *Siobhán Hutson*
Printed in England by imprint*digital*.net

Acknowledgements

These poems represent a triumph of heart – the hearts of many. Although the subject of human trafficking and often the lack of human rights can be disheartening, there are many individuals the resoundingly fight for freedom. This book is dedicated to them – people like Anna Rodriguez (Florida Coalition Against Human Trafficking), Dottie Lassiter (One Million Kids), Mary Shuttleworth (Youth for Human Rights) and so many others who relentlessly work to undo wrongs and make things right.

The creation of a poetry collection always encompasses more energy and deliberation than what I initially conceive. There are so many people who have been of help to create this poem of poems so to speak. I am especially beholden to my wife Shelley who puts up with bouts of moodiness as I comb the universe for words. My family is so very supportive of having a poet in their midst. From my parents to my children I am allowed to poetize spontaneously at any given moment, in fact it is expected.

I would also like to thank Stazja McFadyen my co-founder of Poets for Human Rights for standing up for me when very few did. My great appreciation and admiration to Mary Shuttleworth the President and Founder of Youth for Human Rights – this is one fantastic being. Also my appreciation to Ilya Kaminsky and Sheema Kalbasi for kindly letting writing nice things about me. As for Dottie Lassiter – one of the bravest people I know. She rescues them!

There are a couple of other unsung heroes in this tale and they are Marta Slanska and Jana Jakešova for taking me to camp Terezin and giving me the freedom to sadly explore the streets and cells of this most horrible place. Thankfully, Marta and Jana proceeded to show me the more beautiful parts of Prague and the Czech Republic. I fell in love with Prague that day.

Contents

Speaking of Freedom

FOREWORD BY THE AUTHOR

One child sold is too many. As I sit here and write this, billions and billions are made from the sale of children, women, and men. It is the 21st Century and although slavery has been banished, it is reaching unprecedented heights. Only munitions ranks higher in illicit gains than human trafficking. Unbelievably, it has trumped illegal drugs in the underground commerce. I find this difficult to believe that such an "enlightened" culture still includes human beings as a commodity. Unfortunately, it is so!

In 1948, the United Nations issued the Universal Declaration of Human Rights. The world signed on and adopted it. It is a pity that such a brilliant document has not been followed to the letter. Education is the key to unlocking the riches that this document possesses and can bring to all of mankind. I am privileged to be the official poet for Youth for Human Rights and helping to bring the Declaration back into prominence. It is this knowledge that will help make our world a better place. It is knowledge that will fight ignorance and knowledge that will shine the light of truth upon a world that has gone mad.

The words in this book are from my heart. They represent my care and concern for the wellbeing of everyone. We have the potential to take this planet to great heights of culture and technology. It is the job of the artist to present mankind with an alternative to war and hate. I hope that these works help move us all in the right direction. We can no longer slip away quietly in the darkness. Our survival depends on our responsibility to others and ourselves.

LARRY JAFFE
Poet Laureate Youth for Human Rights
April, 2010

A Note About "One Child Sold"
by ILYA KAMINSKY

"One Child Sold" by Larry Jaffe speaks back to the historical darkness and finding a one's voice not drowned by it. This is a book of many shapes and forms — here are odes, anthems, songs, invocations and narratives. Jaffe writes in a style that reminds us of Langston Hughes' work — in a voice that speaks plainly, simply, with a feeling.

What Jaffe does in this book is to create a lyrical voice that responds to events around him in daily life of America today, events in history, in imagination: lyric as a sounding board for those occurrences. This is also a book of travel, of personal narrative, childhood memory, and song.

The ambition here is to combine the private lyrical voice with the voice that wants to speak for larger political, social and historical issues of justice, discrimination, and fairness. What does it mean to be a poet who speaks for human rights? After all, what poet does not do so? Yet, Jaffe is intent here on creating a figure of a Poet with a capital P, a romantic figure that is nevertheless very plain, an everyman, a poet who speaks on behalf of others in history and in the country of his birth. His ambition is to deal with complex issues of human rights in a simple, plain language of a lyrical invocation.

This need to speak back to history in a private voice of one citizen, one human being, who tries to take on that historical weight and to speak to it in a lyric mode, is instructive. It teaches us about what lyric poetry can and cannot do, and yet it must try to do anyway: to go beyond the boundaries of the genre, to try on an epic ambition, to give a private voice to a larger historical injustice, to speak in humane terms about the horrific events.

In a time when politics of the moment have overwhelmed us with the language of propaganda, it is good to find a private voice of a poet who wants to deal with history in a quieter, humane way. Such ambition should be welcomed. Jaffe, in this volume, clearly believes that there is nothing which cannot be covered in the book of verse, no topic is a taboo. This expansiveness of a lyric voice was what first caught my attention and is what interests me most when I read this book as a fellow writer. I am grateful for the chance to have it.

ILYA KAMINSKY

Introduction by Dottie Laster

I am so honored to introduce *One Child Sold* to readers. Larry Jaffe so vividly and accurately brings the reader into the world of modern slavery and genocide. He lets readers experience the absolute vacuum of human rights with What I Did Today with his description of nothing and his description of the death of the soul while the body is enslaved in *Broken Eyes*.

His phrase "eating broken glass while wearing barbed wire" so accurately describes with words what victims of human bondage can only say in their eyes. Imagine in the United States a child eating the broken glass of molestation and forced prostitution only to wear the barbed wire of being arrested and charged with crimes for being a victim. How in America can children be charged with prostitution when we don't legally recognize their ability to consent to sex with adults? Why are the sex purchasers and pimps often not even detained while victims are handcuffed and prosecuted? We have laws to protect them and charge the true criminals but we need the community to demand a change in perspective. Jaffe's work engages readers to change uninformed societal views surrounding child prostitution and victims of exploiters.

In my work to restore victims and combat human trafficking it has come to my attention how groups or individuals who exploit others can make money where it appears none existed such as the incredible profits of selling a child for sex acts, money made from collecting and selling the personal property of holocaust victims right down to their pairs of shoes, and in whole countries where bondaged labor supports the raping of the minerals, timber, and tourism.

From Sudan, to Myanmar (Burma), to the United States and around the world people are enslaved today for the convenience of diamonds, cheap goods, cheap labor and commercial sex. Everyone can stop this by knowing whose labor you benefit from, reporting activities that seem to restrict workers' freedom of choice and movement, reporting to authorities any minor in commercial sex, and to be aware that trafficked victims are in every country in the world and every state in the United States.

Jaffe's words give the reader the responsibility of knowing that slavery exists and that genocide is not in the past.

Just as the victims of Terezin prayed and hoped for outside help so today pray the victims of modern slavery. Jaffe's words are the beginning of changing the societal mindset that allows slavery and genocide to still exist. This is a disease for all societies until we can be truthful and say 'never again'.

DOTTIE LASTER
Executive Director
Million Kids.org
http://millionkids.org/index.html

Speaking of Human Rights

Human Rights Begin

Where, after all, do Universal Rights begin? In small places, close to home—so close and so small that they cannot be seen on any maps of the world. Yet they are the world of the individual person; farm or office where he works. Such are the places where every man, woman, and child seeks justice, equal opportunity, equal dignity without discrimination. Unless these rights have meaning there, they have little meaning anywhere.

MRS. ELEANOR ROOSEVELT

Human rights begin
with your heart
miraculously transforming
hate to love.

They begin
with your mind
inexplicably converting
fear to courage.

Human rights begin
with your fingers
astonishingly turning
violence into caresses.

They begin
with your family
evolving
ignorance into intelligence

They begin
in your neighborhood
ultimately challenging
prejudice with tolerance.

Human rights begin
wherever you are.

A Renaissance of Human Rights

A house built
of Human Rights
stands aflame

Philosophies assaulted
growing weapons
of prejudice

Buildings fall
like butterflies
in September

Armies held
hostage
proclaiming innocence

Presidents and dictators
take aim
and shoot their own

Worried politicians
shutter rights
in the name of security

Wings are shorn
angels
drop from the sky

From nowhere voices
whisper
neglected freedoms

A child chips
away at pretense
proclaims natural law

The last man standing
cries out
says he is not alone

Citizens defend
30 rights
with vigilance

Freedom reborn
A Renaissance of Human Rights

Everyman

for the Miami Coalition of Christians and Jews

I

A mirror stands
frozen between lives
coated with frost
faces lost unseen.

I dare to look closer
and gaze deeply

—The ice slowly melts

The middle-aged white man
is now timeless
he is no longer white
his skin the color
of everyman

—I wonder
how can I hurt anyone
without hurting myself

II

When I look in this mirror
I see your eyes
& your brother's skin

It is not that we are one
it is that we share
our planet and destiny

—This mirror simply reflects our eternity.

The echoes are blind
they reach to everyone

Hemorrhaging

The Earth bleeds
we stand around
hands in pockets
some shout retaliation
some scream futility
still the earth bleeds

We proclaim peace
accuse each other
march and protest
hold hands for inner warmth
love one another with venom
still the earth bleeds

We kill songs with rocks
torture memories
plead sides
and wonder
why the Earth
still bleeds

—Some never learn to hate

Peace is not a tourniquet
Peace is a new Earth.

Speaking of Human Trafficking

Owned

I am owned
by silence
possessed by others
slavery denied
in the highest places

I am owned
by intolerance
drugs prevent protest
women & children sold
to the highest bidder
on hidden street corners
of underground slave markets

I am owned
by indifference
tears my only salvation
children shackled to machinery
in third-world factories
owned by first-world corporations.

I am owned
by finance
body and soul
women chained to beds
in nomadic brothels

I am owned
by ignorance
my rights abused
invisible chains
bind my soul
you say slavery is dead
I am living proof it lives

I am owned
& only wish
to be free!

I am owned
& will be free!

Caravan to Nowhere

Once they were through
processing the women
girls no bigger than your thumb
tiny girls looking for work
and a way out
not so smart girls
and brilliant girls
young women
really
but more like
girls
they were put to work

They were promised
the big time
the show
how they could
make lots of money
be famous
drink whiskey
and drive
huge automobiles

They wanted
that western
fame & fortune
thing
more than they wanted
life
so they were put to work
sacrificing
everything
getting nothing

They danced
with the merrymen

sang them songs
and did other things
that were not to their
heart's delight
nor any other
part of them

The freedom
the life
they had before
was no more
there is a difference
between
a hard life
and one
that is cruel
tainted with the taste
of metal
and the feel
of barbwire

All because of the
Promise
when they
climbed into that van
scampered on to that boat
leaped into the abyss
of poisoned pledge
of fatuous riches
and private glory

They found themselves
puppets of subjugation
slaves of the 21st century
landlocked captivity
without escape

—Bondage
a caravan to nowhere

Some say they are gullible
some say they are naïve
whatever they are
they are no more
ground into human
snowflakes
precipitating the heat
that destroys them
dispersed with the wind
they wished
the caravan had wings

Rifles

Rifles are not made
for 10 year old hands

Nor triggers for
10 years old fingers

Pistols are too
damn heavy

Dynamite fits
neatly in backpacks

Making
human bombs

Another childhood
memory…

Dreams Are Not Enough

What Color Is Slavery?

Slavery is the color
Of shadows
When the unsuspecting
Are easily surprised
And bellies are empty

Slavery tastes like rust
The bitter metal
Of shackles
On the tongue

Slavery feels like
Eating broken glass while wearing
Barbed wire

Slavery is the color
Of ignorance
The death of the soul
Do not embrace
It

Slaves Do Not Get the Weekend Off

It may be Friday
but slaves
have to work
tomorrow
and the next day
and the day
after that

They get no
days off
no paid
vacation
or free
medical
treatment

They get
no 401K's
or pension
or even
a gold watch
for meritorious
service

There
is no such thing
as slave
benefits
or perks.

There is
no golden
parachute
only a
dirty shroud

Slaves work
till they drop
then swept
away
as garbage

Trash Day
is Thursday
they do
get that
day off.

Wearing Tragedy

Her face is painted the color of heartbreak.
She wears the tragedy of mothers of dead children.
She dresses in the color of mothers of the lost.
Milk spills from her full breasts.
She is nondenominational.

Emptiness

the chair sits
empty
alone
four legs
gripping the floor

Speaking of Terezin

A Few Words About Concentration Camp Terezin

Terezin was the "showplace" concentration camp. As if such a concept could even be conceivable, but indeed that is what it was. The Nazis took the distinguished members of the Red Cross to show them the "Fuhrer's gift to the Jews." It was a "model" ghetto and concentration camp with many artists, writer, musicians, actors and Jewish intelligentsia sent there.

I went to Terezin in May 2006. I labor on this manuscript with visions of hell still visiting. I do not know how a civilization can manifest itself out of these ashes. Nevertheless, I want to offer some hope to the world. Volumes and volumes have been written about the holocaust and there is stagnation in writing about death. Then there are those who claim the holocaust did not exist. They have not walked these trembling halls as I have where the soul is so depleted even after half a century.

> From my blog, I quote: I visited evil today. Evil that lingers in the land and is nurtured by automated hate. The concentration camp at Terezin although a memorial to those that suffered suffers. The air lacks oxygen; if we did not need a reminder of the holocaust and the inhumanity it brings forth I would recommend nuking the entire town. The pain is embedded into the walls. This is not a nice place. It is not a holy place.
>
> But the miracle of Terezin is the art that does remain. The captives of Terezin fought death with art and it is a living tribute to those beings that they could create under such conditions. Simply amazing!
>
> While walking through the museum in Terezin, I saw a copy of a sign found in Belzec, where they sent some of the persons from Terezin. I refuse to write victims or prisoners or even people. I refer to the individuals who were there as persons, individual beings so as not to dehumanize any further what took place there. Belzec was one of several extermination camps.

Belzec was transformed into an even more hideous evil when a camouflaged 'tube,' was installed. It ran from the undressing barracks directly to the gas chambers.

The sign was hanging on a wall in the museum at Terezin even though it was from Belzec. This was right after reading the directive for the destruction of all Jews from May 1942. Even as I write this tears drip down my face. The sign read as follows:

Attention: Completely undress... Hold on to money, valuables and Identification Cards until turning them into the window. Shoes must be tied in pairs and left at the designated location. Then go undressed to the spa and inhalation.

Words have left me. If you ever wonder why I do what I do and have dedicated my life to human rights, just read this sign once again.

Sidebar: I stripped naked and took the hottest and then coldest of showers after I got to my flat. I immediately put everything I was wearing into the wash. I would have burned these clothes so horrid is the stench I feel permeated them in the camp.

One of the books I picked up in Terezin is a book entitled ... *I never saw another butterfly...* written and illustrated by the children of Terezin. It is a magnificent volume and should be read by everyone. More than 15,000 children were sent to this camp, less than 100 survived. This book is dedicated to the children of Terezin

I said before that I want to give hope because where there is life there is hope. I compose this book with fingers that touched the walls, the gates and the poor souls who suffered there. I will not let them be forgotten. I will write of their love and passion. I will work with my friends to prevent it from happening again.

The Children of Terezin

When I visited Camp Terezin
the children called to me
they left ethereal homes
dropped blankets
and held out their tiny hands
for me to lift them up
and hold them close.

I hugged every one of them
as they told me
of Terezin and how
their fairy-tales kept them
alive until story time was over.

I hugged every one of them
as they told me how
they painted pictures
with their fingers
dipped in their mothers' blood.

I hugged every one of them
as they sang songs
and told me nursery rhymes

I hugged every one of them
as they told me about
the playground of graves
how they played hopscotch
over tombstones
and ring around a rosey
was truth

ashes ashes
all fall down

only when they fell down
they never got up.

I hugged every one of them
even the lost soul
who crossed himself
like a gentile
when he cried.

I hugged every one of them
because the children of Terezin
no longer wait for their mothers
to call them home

Today they have been set free.

Terezin Blue

In Terezin
the souls so broken
they are afraid
to go home.

In Terezin
the souls so terrified
they cannot
recycle their goodness.

They fear there are insufficient
new bodies to accommodate
them and recycle their goodness.

They wonder in disquieted enlightenment
should they stay in Terezin as reminders
or reemerge in corporal form.

A mixture of dread
of not wanting
to be forgotten
yet afraid
to remember.

What I Did Today

Today I had nothing
except the scraps
of food scraps
that no longer
stick to bones
or builds bodies
in any way.

Today I had nothing
perhaps I can fashion model
the skin and bones look
is in this year…
but there is no runway
for models
or airplanes
there is no leaving
except as ancestor.

Today I had nothing
the cold is vibrant
but does not make you feel alive
our clothing a patchwork
carnival of cloth
that barely gives shelter
we all look alike
males and females
heads shaved
for the wig factory.

Today I had nothing
the bricks of the walls
do not show the
tears that built it
the wind never
stops howling
there is no justice or mercy

only cracks in concrete
to remind us of the frailty.

Today I had nothing
and wonder why me
and ask god for forgiveness
if he would just set me free
I would believe in him
instead I watch others
look for signs and omens
betraying god's existence
or is it his ignorance.

Today I had nothing
and realize I feel
spiritually barren
my faith no
longer good company
I rail against a god
that no longer exists
I would gladly trade
my dignity for food.

Today I had nothing
even the muse
left me and
I can no longer
write in blood
on these concentration
camp walls
my blood has gone dry.

Today I have nothing…

Cattle Car

Dedicated to the Jewish Warring Organisation who resisted tyranny

"In addition to the harm the warriors wanted to inflict on the enemy they wanted to show the world that in spite of their isolation the Jews resisted the Nazi murder machine. It was important to show that the Jews did not go like lambs to the slaughter. In Poland the history of this event was recorded as a rebellion act executed by the Gwardia Ludowa... Jewish warriors were not mentioned even once in spite of the fact that not even one Pole participated. The Germans also contributed to the historical distortion by never admitting in public to the Jewish rebellion."

I cannot see myself boarding a train to oblivion
a rail to nowhere going along with the herd for a ride

I cannot see myself despite my Jewishness
going into a cattle car under anyone's volition
let alone my own

I cannot see myself riding the rails of a cattle car
packed inside like human sardines and someone else
holds the keys to my future

I cannot see myself climbing into the car
nor letting my family climb in this car
without a fight

I see disheveled disoriented Jews going
for a ride, one-way tickets clutched in
hands not made of fists...

—they travel to Auschwitz or Buchenwald

I wonder about the travel agent that sold these tickets
and the tour guide from hell that gave them the ride
I cannot see vacationing in Poland as a holiday

This was not Noah's ark it was Hitler's ark, Nazi's ark

—They were not taking two of every species
they were taking six million of one

But I cannot see myself walking calmly without a fight,
suffering the dishonor of mental dismemberment
slowly to holocaust away.

—Number tattoos are not rosebuds or nametags

—Some say you were not there I say I was and am reborn
yet again…

This was death camp and I do not hear cries of joy,
only the sounds of vultures parading in goosesteps.

But the Nazis were very polite in their violence
their uniforms crisply cut bleeding the fingers
that clutched them.

The camps so spotless and scrubbed
even the ovens were self-cleaning
I wonder who made them.

The Nazis so well spoken— relocation they preached,
the ghetto is so dirty, scour your soul, clean up your act—
take a shower in this stall without drains

They said it so politely—

Very few resisted and went willingly
going on one-way holiday, bags packed
with all perishables

Where were the men
Where were the women
as mankind and children were
merchandised and victimized?

They were just following orders
the Nazis were just following orders
the Jews were just following orders
today's Nazis are still following orders

I cannot see myself following orders
I will not follow orders.

Speaking of Freedom

Anthem

Listen closely
you can still hear the sound
of the third Reich marching

Listen as
boots jackhammer
across pavements and boardrooms

Listen as
crowds shout in streets
as terror rises from
asphalt paved with bones

Listen as
Hitler's screams
rise from the tombs
hear the death rattle

Sieg Heil
(jackhammer boots march on asphalt)

Sieg Heil
(arms goose step)

Sieg Heil
(boots click heels)

Sieg Heil
(arms shoot up)

Sieg Heil
(boots click heels)

—There is challenge to the darkness

as serenity forms
and understanding
no longer takes
a back seat

Grief stricken relatives
should no longer hold hands
they should shun excuses
and build fists
of understanding
as

One being stands up
then another
and another...

L'Chaim
(arms pump fists)

L'Chaim
(arms never waver)

L'Chaim
(we never give up)

L'Chaim
L'Chaim
L'Chaim

Darkess at Darfur

—never again
—never again
—never again

When I was young
this mantra
of never again
never again
never again
was drummed
into my eyes
ears
nose
& throat

—never again
never again
keeps happening ever again

They say the never
ending sun in Darfur
never sets yet why
is it always dark?

Bodies carelessly
bent, mislaid
souls displaced
—never again

Publicity spins
brave new words
presidents pompous
finger pointing
dictators dancing
masters of chicanery
feudal frauds

their mouths lying
for public order
only to feed
their arduous ardor.

They fail to remember
that the hangman's
noose swings both ways

—never again
—never again
—never again

Our Flag Flies Free

for the Shan Relief Foundation & the Shan People

I wear the flag
of yellow, green & red
touched
by purest white.

I am Shan
Our Flag Flies Free

Beauty lost
in revolt of righteous
monks replaced
with military precision

We are Shan
We shine once more

To be Shan
is to be free
the shallow grave
of slavery swallows
us no more.

We are Shan
We are Free

I wear the yellow
for the spirit
that bends
but never breaks.

I wear the green
for the land
forever verdant
and alive.

I wear the red
for the courage
to protect our families
and each other .

And gracing the center
of our Shan soul
peace,
purity
tranquility.

We are the Shan
Our Flag Flies Free

Walking in Sand

I have walked the sands
in feet of Muslim and Jew.

One lifetime I wear the Kufi
and the next the Yarmulke
from wandering Jew
to ready Muslim.

I march through endless desert
flag erect , mind besotted
with unrequited loathing
strangling in righteousness.

It is difficult to keep
track of which lifetime
I despise the most
Muslim or Jew
in perpetual motion
pressure of unseen fingers.

I change religions
like vestments
representing each lifetime
worn by the
mullahs and rabbis before me.

Each lifetime
I undress in the sand
trying to understand
the lifetime before me.

I live in endless revulsion
wondering why brothers fight
breeding hate
with the brilliance
of genetic engineering

surrendering our offspring
to eternal death.

And I wonder if I live
through enough lifetimes
will I finally understand
who really designs this war.

Will I at last identify
those perpetrators of chaos
to brave souls
and will they finally stop
waving their banners
like electrified sex symbols .

It is my final wish
for them to fly
their flags of hate
at half-mast
while I watch love
bloom in the sand.

War Zone

The Statue of Liberty wears a
dress of tattered barbed wire
her wounds are dressed
with plastic explosives.
If they cannot have liberty
no one can.

—It is very difficult to love your enemy
and simultaneously prepare for war.

Does precious balance teeter
when 3000 lives die on each side?
Is there a minimum death quota
by which we all feel avenged?

I don't know which hurts more
the dissolution of the illusion of peace
or the pretense of being a pacifist.

Tear-Stained Cuffs

I watched this young black man
wearing tear-stained handcuffs
knowing that if he had my white face
his wrists would not
be covered in iron.

It was just a quick drive-by viewing
cop car's lighting up twilight sky
like fourth of July.

Two LA gendarmes led the fray of one
young black man manacled to himself
so he could do nobody harm
standing there like a poster boy
for political violations.

He drank in their eyes and scowls
—bloodlines curdling his vision

This young man ventured out of his playground
into some white stucco neighborhood
that I always thought was mixed

He looked up at me with eyes half full of tears
speckled with futility and defiance
as if to say:

> can you see yourself wearing so
> much official jewelry?

Threaded through stocks of public humiliation
crying hard tears of frustration,
his eyes were not running
they were caught in the headlamps of
the American law machine
to witness cuffs chained to bone.

Implanted with the unwillingness
to change perceptions
open eyes
and live a little
perhaps
let others live a little

Arise Slaves

Are we not all slaves
beholden to work and ruler
that only take
or give too much
from self-proclaimed divinity
declaring dependence
when what we really seek
is independence?

Are we not all slaves
to thoughts and notions
taking umbrage
at verbal onslaughts
and physical manifestation
and now dethroned
from the pinnacle
we mourn our destiny
venturing in denial.

Are we not all slaves
to our own ignorance
of people and places
losing bearing
and orientation
to a secretive compass
that controls the stars
our supposed eternity

Are we not all slaves
waiving impotent rights
to a lesser champion
when the one we seek
resides within us
calling out
to break these chains
of betrayal.

Are we not all slaves
pounding doors
rattling chains
and manacles
as fashion statement
mutated fetters confining
spirit and imagination.

Are we not all slaves
to fad, desire, peers
and pressures.

Slowly relieving themselves
of these tentacles
of uncivilization
emancipation
unfolds and blooms.

A Pause, A Tear, A Flower

1

He is empathic and feels for people
the very core of their emotions
reaching into him screaming

The pain so strong
envelops, surrounds
and overwhelms.
He is a radio receiver
tuned into suffering

He cries

He cries for things
he cannot see
and things he sees too clearly

He cries because
of the pain in his heart
and never ending pain
in his bones

He cries for children
growing hungry
for women abused
by a society of militants.

He cries for soldiers
fighting for lost causes
substituting bravery
for honor.

He cries for police beating
society into oblivion
and criminals shredding
values vital.

He cries for humanity

2

He is empathic
and broadcasts joy
to every passerby.

The pain so strong
envelops, surrounds
and overwhelms.
He is a radio receiver
tuned into suffering

He loves everyone
embraces them
reaches out laughing

The pleasure so powerful
it caresses every soul
he is a broadcaster
radiating pleasure

The day is beautiful,
the sun shining so brightly
it almost blinds

Children laugh and play
in streets of concrete
and sweat

Mothers and fathers gaze
fondly at offspring
life eventually triumphs.

Lovers walk hand in hand

He smiles for humanity.

Suburban

I was raised in suburbia
without stigmata
Jews and Christians roamed
a land once inhabited
by cucumbers, wheat and potatoes.

The wheat became white bread
as did the schools and playgrounds
but soon the fields were no more.

We grew up to the sounds
of Frankie Valley
who taught us to walk like a man
even though we were boys.

We played soldier killing krauts & nips
We played cowboys and Indians
I always wanted to be the Indian
Native American Jew.

We learned to kiss at parties
playing games of post office &
spin the bottle.

Not once did we play
CIVIL RIGHTS LEADER OR
FRIEND.

Our mothers taught
us to get along
with each other
and not be harbingers
of secret hates.

Except the boy down
the street had parents who hated
Jews
&
Negroes.

There were no Negroes
In the neighborhood
so they centered
their hate on the Jews.

My mother did not understand
ANTI-SEMITISM. She spoke
perfectly pure ghetto before
it was popular.

But that did not stop
the Nazis from being intolerant.
The only museums they had
were dedicated to KRISTALLNACHT
a night of pogrom.

What's a mother to do?

Today when I think of the holocaust
I see the bodies piled like timber wood
and the sweetish smell of burning flesh.
The stripping of consciousness
along with gold fillings and JEWelry.

But mom did not know that the people
down the street hated her because of her blood
and the hate hand-me-downed to their offspring
who wore HH tattooed on his red-haired forehead.
He prevailed with that hate through 12 years of school.

Today a President of Iran says the holocaust
never happened. I challenge him to walk with me
through my childhood and through the streets of
Terezin. Perhaps he can come with me to Auschwitz.
I will make sure he takes out his nose filters &
earplugs, removes his blindfold.
Perhaps then he can see the products of hate
and that last lifetime he might have been a Jew in Poland.

Small Victories

I sit at a lunch counter
in the South reading a sign
proclaiming quality food
since 1965,
red-vinyl stools twirl
for hungry passengers.

The restaurant
does not
smell as greasy
as some I have
visited
in the past.

There are two Black
school girls,
one Asian woman,
one Black woman,
2 Black men,
4 White men,
2 White women,
1 Jewish man
and one more or less
Off-White guy
sitting at that counter.

The school girls
order burgers, fries
and cokes
they wait hungrily.

One of the White
men is mighty
immense,
he looks
as if he eats well.

One of the White women
who is hard of hearing
shouts at no one
in particular
while her son
hides behind
the menu.

An elderly white man
talks haphazardly
about the weather
to a young Black
woman.

I wonder
what it was
like in 1965?

Broken Eyes

My eyes are broken
they tire from
relentless
bashing of principles

They wanted to see
what they should
not see
and broke
irrevocably sad

The fire that
once fed my belly
has gone out
replaced by
damp spirits

Now the kindred
fly lame
without wonder
transmitting disdain

I wanted to envision
peace and found war
my eyes cried
until even
the tears dried

I have learned
to confront the world
with my stupidity
and nakedness
this was my legacy

I was a fallen angel
without a god
to inspire me

I turned myself
inside out
removing the skin
from the soul

And without effort
I now see
without eyes
touch without fingers
and laugh
and laugh

I am no longer
a body
and soar like
an eagle
sans wings

I am a free spirit
engaged in the
most gentle
of intercourses
the world is my wonder

We will heal the disease
end the mayhem of war
calm the troubled
and bring joy to the sad
this is our legacy

Just Routine

It was just routine
a visit to the doctor
while suffering from
heartbreak
medicine prescribed
no healing
for broken hearts.

Sadness lingers
diagnosis
from psych book
of superstitions
must be
unrequited love
syndrome
—more drugs

Sadness
a thing of the past
apathy deepens
and feelings melt
from bones
squeezed like
venom
—more drugs

No longer sad
a zombie
rests on
suicidal perch
waiting
for voices
to call home
—more drugs

no therapy
no religion
only heresy
of oath
one day
realization
that sadness
is better
than nothing
feeling is
better
than nothing

no more visits
to impenetrable medicos
no more drugs
instead a walk
on the beach
when feeling sad
it does wonders...

Earth Song

She listens
to earth softly
eyes
moisture
mourning dew.

She sings
earth eternal
gently leaning
to earth rhythms
—her harmony.

She plays
earth song
like rhapsody
engaging each moment
in symphony.

What Would Happen

what would happen
if I could remember your
memories
instead of my own

what would happen if our touch
was more than umbilical
our lives parallel
vertical interchanged with versatility
relaxed with reality
a merger of souls sparked
with natural blossoms and fireworks
every touch fourth of July
every kiss atomic
every sensual moment nuclear

what would happen if
we were not exposed
to shamelessness
and preserved ourselves
for deity

what would happen
if our poses were
discreet smiles
that said mouthfuls
and our eyes always met

what would happen if we
were only friends but
wanted to feel just as
close as lovers

what would happen
if we were kindred
spirits that speared universes
gathered no moss
and rolled to victory

You

You are a wonder
a maker of miracles
the essence of life
the moods that strike
are not you.

You are your own messiah
your own soul
you are it
the beauty
not the aftermath
not the cargo.

You are truth
life reborn
again and again
in spiritual splendor
not the shell
of one lifetime.

You are you
from a sacred shower
you emerge
unguarded
uncloaked
a faint halo.

—YOU

About the author

Larry Jaffe has been using his art to promote human rights throughout his entire professional career.

He is the Poet Laureate for Youth for Human Rights and the former Poet in Residence at the Autry Museum of Western Heritage. Jaffe has been featured in poetry venues and festivals both throughout the U.S. and abroad in such distinguished locations as the Japanese American Museum, Hammer Museum, the Jewish Museum and the Museum of Literature in Prague and the Dylan Thomas Centre in Wales. His work has been translated into over a dozen languages. Jaffe was the recent recipient of the Saint Hill Art Festival's Lifetime of Creativity Award, the first time given to a poet.

Jaffe served as International Readings Coordinator for the UNESCO Dialogue among Civilizations through Poetry Project from 2001 to 2004, a project that incorporated hundreds of readings in hundreds of cities globally. He is also the co-founder of Poets for Human Rights, an international coalition of poets and human rights advocates with chapters all over the world.

From the sensually romantic to humor and social commentary, Larry Jaffe impacts audiences with a rich emotional range, masterfully crafted. His poetry appears in numerous anthologies, magazines, and on the Internet where he has pioneered poetry communities and web sites.